Barnyard Animals

Sheep on a Farm

Abbie Mercer

PowerKiDS press
New York

For Kai Uhlin

Published in 2010 by The Rosen Publishing Group, Inc.
29 East 21st Street, New York, NY 10010

First Edition

Editor: Amelie von Zumbusch
Book Design: Kate Laczynski
Photo Researcher: Jessica Gerweck

Photo Credits: Cover, pp. 1, 7, 9, 11, 13, 15, 19, 21, 24 (flock, pasture, ram) Shutterstock.com; p. 5 © www.istockphoto.com; pp. 17, 24 (hay) © www.istockphoto.com/Gene Krebs; p. 23 Kevin Hatt/Getty Images.

Library of Congress Cataloging-in-Publication Data

Mercer, Abbie.
Sheep on a farm / Abbie Mercer. — 1st ed.
p. cm. — (Barnyard animals)
Includes index.
ISBN 978-1-4042-8050-2 (library binding) — ISBN 978-1-4042-8061-8 (pbk.) — ISBN 978-1-4042-8062-5 (6-pack)
1. Sheep—Juvenile literature. I. Title. II. Series.
SF375.2.M47 2010
636.3—dc22

2008048084

Manufactured in the United States of America

Contents

Do you know what the soft animal this boy is leading is called? It is a sheep!

Sheep live on farms. They often stay in outdoor **pastures**.

Sheep are known for their thick coats of hair, called wool.

Sheep are most often white. They can also be brown, gray, black, or a mix of these colors.

Male sheep are known as **rams**. Female sheep are called ewes. Baby sheep are lambs.

Lambs are most often born in the spring. They like to run, play together, and take naps.

Young lambs drink their mothers' milk. Older sheep eat grass and **hay**.

Sheep live in groups, called **flocks**. Sheep like to stay near the other members of their flock.

Farmers sometimes use dogs to keep flocks of sheep together.

Farmers often raise sheep for their wool. People make warm clothes, such as sweaters, from wool.

Words to Know

flock

hay

pasture

ram

Index

Web Sites

Due to the changing nature of Internet links, PowerKids Press has developed an online list of Web sites related to the subject of this book. This site is updated regularly. Please use this link to access the list: www.powerkidslinks.com/byard/sheep/